Why
Wasa
Capsized

Curt Borgenstam · Anders Sandström

Wasa Studies 13

Sjöhistoriska museet   Wasa Rediviva

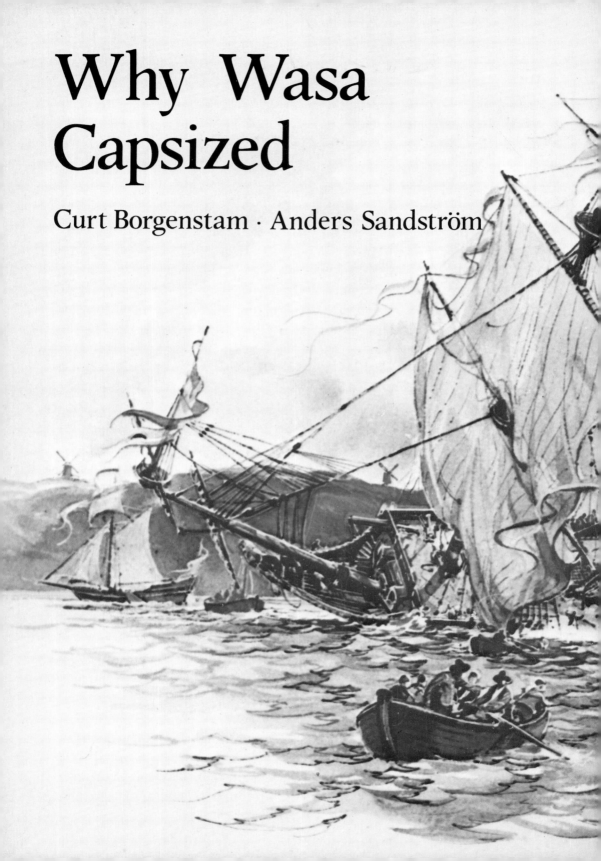

Why Wasa Capsized

Curt Borgenstam · Anders Sandström

Wasa Studies are published by Statens sjöhistoriska museum (National Maritime Museum), Stockholm.
2 000 copies printed.

Editor: Erling Matz
Translation: Curt Borgenstam and Klas Helmerson
Copyright: Statens sjöhistoriska museum
(National Maritime Museum), Stockholm
ISBN 91-85268-23-2

Printed by AB Grafisk Press, Stockholm
Paper 115 g Offblade
Type Times 10/12

The series "Wasa Studies" is published by the Maritime Museum/Wasa Museum in Stockholm and the Wasa Rediviva Foundation. It consists of scientific and popular studies and articles related to the *Wasa*.

During the next few years, activities at the Wasa Museum are mainly concentrated on the building of the new, permanent Wasa Museum, situated a few hundred metres from the present, temporary Museum. Thus, material, published in the series "Wasa Studies" will to a large extent consist of papers, produced as a background for the new exhibitions.

Parallel with the series "Wasa Studies", the publishing of a scientific, analytic catalogue of the finds from the *Wasa* is planned. The first group of objects that has been analysed is the sculptures.

Cover picture: The afternoon of August 10, 1628. The *Wasa* capsizes "with standing sails, flags and all" in the light breeze from the Tegelviken Bay. Water colour by Nils Stödberg.

Contents

Why Did the Wasa Capsize?

Curt Borgenstam

The *Wasa* can be claimed to be the oldest existing ship of the Royal Swedish Navy, but her active life was extremely short. On the 10th of August, 1628, she set out on her maiden voyage, but even before she left Stockholm harbour she capsized in a light squall and sank. In spite of all effort no convincing explanation of the disaster was ever given.

Still today, when the *Wasa* has been found and salvaged, the same question is repeatedly being asked: How could it happen?

Sjöhistoriska museet (the Maritime Museum), the Wasa Rediviva Foundation and independent experts are now in the process of studying and documenting this unique archaeological find.

Since the *Wasa* was salvaged in 1961, her hull has been carefully investigated and measured and a linear drawing has been made. Through the efforts of Captain (E) Gunnar Schoerner, the firm SIKOB has computed stability curves, based on the hull shape, and presented them to the Maritime Museum. Thus we are today in a better position to find an answer to the question put in 1628.

It so happens that I teach "Warship Design" to the Marine Engineering Cadets at the Royal Institute of Technology in Stockholm. As part of the course the students have to do a project study on a chosen subject. For the 1979 course I chose to let my students process stability figures for the *Wasa* which the computer had produced, in such a way that the stability characteristics of the ship could be illustrated.

Soon, it became clear that essential factors were unknown and in all probability would remain so. Although the shape of the hull is known, the weight and distribution of the equipment at the moment of disaster are uncertain factors. Thus, it became necessary both to make certain assumptions and to calculate with several possible alternatives.

The results of the calculations were ready at the end of the course in June, 1979. They have inspired me to attempt to analyse and shed light on the probable course of events during the disaster and on its causes. This has been done on the basis of documents contemporary with the *Wasa*, comparisons with information about shipbuilding at that time and a critical analysis of the records of the hearings. The main part of my studies have been undertaken in 1979 during a short period of leave of absence from my duties at the Defence Materiel Administration. The results have been compiled in the present volume.

In the course of my work, I have studied material concerning the *Wasa*, published earlier by scientists and historians and relating to the question of the capsizing. I was given valuable assistance by several experts who have contributed with points of view on the problem itself, on the methods of attacking it and on the form of presentation of the result.

I have greatly appreciated the cooperation with Björn Landström, Ph.D. His deep knowledge of older naval architecture has been a rich source of information. During my studies, Björn Landström was working at the Wasa Museum, studying the naval architecture of the *Wasa*. This offered us opportunities for thorough discussions, through which Doctor Landström's knowledge greatly enriched my work. His vivid interest and enthusiasm were also an inspiration for me personally.

I have cooperated for a long time with Mr. Anders Franzén, who discovered the wreck of the *Wasa*. Already before he had managed to locate the wreck, Anders Franzén gave me access to his excerpts and notes. They have been of great use to me when studying the archives. As I was in charge of the Machinery and Diving Section at the Stockholm Naval Yard in 1956—57, I became involved in the *Wasa* project at an early stage. This also came natural in view of my longstanding acquaintance with Anders Franzén. Thanks to his well known aptitude for thorough research, he has been of great assistance in the planning of my work.

The Maritime Museum has kindly given me access to all

its material about the *Wasa*. My thanks go especially to its former First Curator, Commander Bengt Ohrelius, who has acted as an efficient point of contact with the experts of the Museum and contributed with useful ideas and suggestions. His experience as a writer has also been of great value, and he has been kind enough to read my manuscripts.

The first naval architect to attempt to study in depth the shipbuilding technique of the *Wasa* was Captain (E) Gunnar Schoerner. At an early stage, he realized what an extraordinary material for study the ship could offer. As a professional naval engineer, he is also familiar with the problems of stability, which constitute a great part of the riddle of the *Wasa* disaster. Captain Schoerner has also contributed with valuable suggestions on the present study, which may be regarded as a continuation of the work that he himself initiated.

Among my students, I should like to mention Mr. Pär Dahlander and Mr. Torbjörn Frisk who have put a great deal of work and dedication into the stability calculations and their presentation. By studies on board the ship and in the Museum archives, Torbjörn Frisk has also helped to throw light on the distribution of ballast and other weights in the ship.

My superiors in the Defence Materiel Administration have contributed by allowing me one month of leave in 1979 to facilitate my studies.

To all those who have helped me in different ways I want to extend my sincere thanks for a positive and pleasant cooperation. It is my hope that this study will contribute to the solution of an old mystery and inspire to further research in this field.

Täby in April, 1984
Curt Borgenstam

Background

When the sunken warship *Wasa* was located by Anders Franzén in 1956 and subsequently salvaged, Sweden was provided not only with a unique tourist attraction and a cultural memorial, but also with an interesting and valuable object for research in the field of shipbuilding technology. No drawings have been preserved from 17th centry shipbuilding — indeed, no drawings in the proper sense of the word were ever produced, not even as guidelines for the construction.

Measurement specifications were used, but those were what we today would call "rules of the thumb". They were tables of figures, giving the various measures of a ship. The

measurement specifications and dimensions of the *Wasa* have earlier been dealt with by, among others, Captain Gunnar Schoerner on the basis of measurings of the hull and comparisons with literary information about naval architecture of that time. From this, it becomes evident that the shape of the *Wasa's* "master frame section" (corresponding to the midship section of a modern ship) very closely follows the so called Dutch school (this, and the English school represent the two most widely used methods of establishing the dimensions at that time). This can easily be explained by the fact that the Master Shipwright of the *Wasa* was a Dutchman, immigrated to Sweden.

The paper by Anders Sandström "The *Wasa* and the King's Specification" in this volume will present a more detailed analysis of the specifications and the building history of the two large warships, the *Wasa* and the *Tre Kronor*.

Contemporary pictures of ships show only the exterior and are often very incorrect. Of the *Wasa*, no picture at all exists. The salvage of the *Wasa* offered first opportunity to study in detail the design and construction of a 17th century ship.

An Ideal Wreck

Anders Franzén has described the *Wasa* as "the ideal wreck". When she foundered, she was brand new and

A master shipwright and his wife. He is holding a pair of compasses, on the table is a footstick and a drawing of a master frame. Etching by Rembrandt.

Anders Franzén boards the Wasa after the raising in April, 1961. This was 333 years after she sank and five years after Anders Franzén had located the ship.

in good condition. Still after three hundred years, her wooden hull was unaffected by rot and teredo worms. The depth at the site of the wreck was only about 30 metres and the place is sheltered, which facilitated the search for and the salvage of the ship. It was

The Wasa is by no means the only ship to capsize in port. Here, the British ship-of-the-line Royal George founders off Spithead in 1782.

only a few hundred metres from the Naval Yard — thus all technical facilities were within easy reach. Altogether, conditions were unusually favourable for the salvage which was subsequently undertaken with the combined resources of the Navy and the Neptun Salvage Company.

From the point of view of cultural and shipbuilding history, the untimely ending of the *Wasa's* maiden voyage might be regarded as a lucky event, but at the time when she went down, it was a major disaster and a blow to the Navy. Therefore, steps were immediately taken, albeit without success, to find out what had caused the accident. Was the ship incompetently handled or maneuvred? Did she carry too large or too many sails? Was she overloaded? Was there anything wrong in her design or construction?

It should be emphasised that capsizings were not unusual. Even a quick look at the tall stern super-

structures and the hulls, narrowing upwards, hints that stability was often dubious, especially after the guns had begun to be placed on more than one deck for greater artillery effectiveness.

Understanding of the concept of stability was rather vague and calculations of the problem were completely unknown. It was up to the officers of each ship to try to find out her stiffness and to try out how to sail it and what sails to carry in various winds. However, it is interesting to note that a stability test was carried out with the *Wasa* at the quay, even though the methods of measurement and the evaluation of the results left much to be desired.

Obviously, the *Wasa* was a "crank" ship with insufficient stability. But just *how* bad her stability was and *what* caused the deficiencies is a rather complicated question.

The Inquiries

To find the clues to the solution of the mystery there are two fields where additional information is to be found. One is the partly restored ship itself, even if great parts of its equipment, armament and rigging are missing. The other is the records from the inquiries held after the disaster. These records are still preserved in the War Archives and the National Archives. They can yield useful information not only regarding the actual equipment and armament of the *Wasa* when she sailed, but also of the very special conditions that prevailed during her construction and fitting out. We shall start by examining them.

Admittedly, the records cannot give a complete picture. In the record from the main inquiry held on the 5th of

The inquiry was held at the Tre Kronor Palace in Stockholm. This print by Erik Dahlberg from his book "Svecia Antiqua et Hodierna" shows the palace a few decades later than the Wasa. Preceding page: A vision by Hjalmar Molin (1868—1954) of the palace in the 17th century.

Captain Söfring Hansson had been right. The guns had not shifted over and caused the capsizing. The guncarriages were in place when the Wasa was raised.

Sept 1628, the introductory part is missing. The notes are also somewhat fragmentary. The secretaries have simply not had time to write down what was said, and it must often have been hard for them to follow the professional expressions of the various experts. We must also keep in mind that the interrogators were aiming not only at clarifying the cause of the capsizing, but also at finding those responsible. Thus the testimonies were given under direct threat of severe punishment, and the penalties were harsh. In many cases the threat was very strongly and openly expressed. The interrogator often started his questioning by accusing the witness: "that he had not let it be known that the ship was crank", "that he had not shown the vigilance which

his office had called for", "that he had possibly been drunk", "that the ship had been narrow and badly built". The witnesses would thus have had good reason and inclination to conceal or twist the facts.

The Inquiries of the 11th of August

Immediately after the disaster the surviving Captain, Söfring Hansson, was arrested and put in prison. Already the day after, the 11th of August, a preliminary inquiry was held with him and the shipbuilder.

The fact that the *Wasa* capsized very quickly must at the outset have given rise to the suspicion that the gun carriages had not been properly secured. These were fitted with wheels, and if the tackles securing them to the side were too slack, the windward guns might roll over to lee when the ship started to heel for the wind. Such a shifting of weight would of course have caused the ship to capsize. But this was a well known problem. Captain Söfring Hansson swore that all cannon were well lashed: "... and if one single cannon was not lashed then they may cut him in a thousand pieces..." In this he was also correct, for when the *Wasa* was raised 333 years later, all the gun carriages were found to stand at their proper place. The Captain also swore that everybody on board had been sober.

Questioned about the stability, he said: "...Ballast was there as much as there was room for, and 100 lasts more than Admiral Fleming wanted, and the ship was so tender that she could not carry her masts...".

The King, Gustaf II Adolf, was leading the campaign overseas against Poland, so he had to be informed by letter the next day, the 12th of August 1628, that his brand new and much longed for ship, the *Wasa,* had capsized and was lying on the bottom of Stockholm harbour! However, he was consoled by the message that an Englishman, by name of Ian Bulmer, had already been entrusted to raise her. He did start his efforts next day.

The Inquiries of the 5th of September

On the 5th of September 1628, a Naval Court of Inquiry was set up to interrogate all those who were supposed to have any information leading to the clarification of the disaster. The court was composed of 17 persons, 6 of whom were members of the Council of the Realm. The King's half brother, Admiral Karl Karlsson Gyllenhielm, was acting as a chairman.

The inquiry did not yield any conclusive result regarding the cause of the disaster, and no one was found guilty. After the inquiry a group of the experts of the court assembled in order to analyse the records and try to arrive at an explanation. From this meeting also there is a preserved record.

The Lord Admiral Karl Karlsson Gyllenhielm, half brother of King Gustav Adolf, presided at the inquiries.

Planning and Building the Wasa

The Naval Shipyard in Amsterdam at the end of the 17th century. The Wasa was built in the Dutch manner by the Master Shipwright Henrik Hybertsson. (Ludolf Backhuysen 1631—1708).

During the period from 1621 to 1625, work at the Naval Yard was directed by Antonius Monier with Henrik Hybertsson, a Dutchman by origin, as an employed shipbuilder. On January 16, 1625, a new contract of lease for the shipyard was signed, this time with the two brothers Henrik and Arend Hybertsson. They complemented each other very well. Henrik was a naval architect while Arend was a businessman having good contacts with subsuppliers both in Sweden and in Holland. Arend Hybertsson was often called de Groot or Degroot (The Grand or The Big). The contract included the construction of four ships: two smaller with a keel length of about 108 feet and two larger of 135 feet. A detailed account of the contract can be found in the paper by Anders Sandström in this volume, page 60.

After a few years the finances of the shipyard began to cause problems. Among other things, this came to delay the construction of the *Wasa*, and in the end the work on the *Wasa* was characterized by great haste and improvisations. Another effect was increased tension between Arend Hybertsson and his customer, the Navy. The conflicts culminated in the *Wasa* disaster. Shortly after this, Arend Hybertsson relinquished his rights as a burgher in Stockholm and left secretly for Holland. Many years later he returned to Sweden, but that is another story.

The Plans are Changed

The newbuilding plans from early 1625 were however changed, following the loss of no less than ten Navy ships in a storm in September of the same year. King Gustaf Adolf, then with his army in Germany, was so alarmed by this that he wrote to Admiral Klas Fleming on the 4th of November, asking him to make certain that Master Henrik will soon start the construction of the two smaller ships, thereby to some extent covering the losses.

But what is meant by "smaller"? Oddly enough, the King seems to have been personally engaged, not only in the artillery, but also in shipbuilding. In his letter to Fleming, he enclosed his own measurement specifications. There, he gives the dimensions of the ship: keel length 120 feet and bottom beam 24 feet.

This caused new problems for Henrik Hybertsson, as the King's specifications would give a ship, whose size would be between those of the larger and smaller ships planned. Dimensions would not match with the timber, which had long since been felled for the original ships.

On the 22nd of February, the King again wrote to Admiral Fleming that his specifications were to be followed. If Master Henrik was not willing or able to follow them, he was instead to build the larger ship (that is, with a keel length of 135 feet). One month later, the King's instructions were conveyed to Hybertsson, who wrote in his answer that the ship "now under construction" would be somewhat shorter than His Majesty had wanted, but she would still be a good ship.".

This implies that Master Henrik intended to build a ship of 108 feet, one that would be smaller than that of

On the stocks. From the book "Om skeppsbyggeri" (On Shipbuilding) by Rålamb, 1691.

120 feet, contained in the King's specifications. If the ship "now under construction" was the *Wasa*, and everything points to this, then it seems as though Master Henrik has later tried to comply with the King's wish for a larger ship: the keel length of the *Wasa* is actually 135 feet. But the keel is constructed from four pieces, joined by three scarf joints, which is said to be more than usual. It might be that Hybertsson, in order to satisfy the King, has constructed a ship of 135 feet, even though bottom and keel for a 108 feet ship had already been laid.

These changes might have influenced her stability, and the frequently altered plans clearly show the confusion which has obviously been prevalent from the very beginning of the planning and construction of the *Wasa*.

The Shipbuilder Falls Sick

Henrik Hybertsson did not live to see the completion and the sad end of the *Wasa*. Towards the end of 1625 he got seriously ill. His condition worsened and he died in the spring of 1627. The continued work on the *Wasa* had to be taken over by his assistant, Hein Jacobsson, who also was born a Dutchman.

During this transition period the shipbuilding management of the *Wasa* project was weak. The responsibility was divided between the sick Henrik Hybertsson and his assistant, the latter most probably having difficulties in finding out what he could decide on his own and what his sick boss wanted to be consulted about.

Nowadays a building contract always contains a detailed description of the ship, its design, execution and required performance, which both parts, the supplier and the customer, have agreed upon. The case of the *Wasa* was quite different. The description in the Hybertsson contract is very scanty. It only gives the length and the beam, and even these dimensions were, as we have seen, later altered.

The Prototype for the Wasa

In his testimony Henrik Hybertsson's brother Arend mentions a kind of "lead ship" or prototype for the *Wasa*, which he says "had been built according to the specification which he had contracted with the King after he had shown him a French ship built in Holland for Duc de Guise". Obviously he wanted to convince the Court of Inquiry that the *Wasa* was similar to this French ship,

According to Arend Hybertson, a "prototype" for the Wasa had been shown to the King. There are many indications that he referred to this engraving by Henrik Hondius of the French ship Saint Louis.

A shipyard in the 17th century, drawn by the Dutch Cornelius van Yk. Facing page: detail from the same picture. A carpenter at work with an auger (large borer).

and also that the King himself had approved it.

The background to this is extensively told and described by Captain Georg Hafström, who came to the conclusion that the ship Arend Hybertsson claimed to have shown to the King was most probably the French warship *Saint Louis*. This was the biggest of a group of ships ordered by the French to be built in Holland, but which were retained there for a long time because of the Dutch Government's fears for opposition from England, the principal enemy of France. The artist Henrik Hondius made an engraving of the *Saint Louis*, which became one of the most widespred and frequently copied illustrations of a 17th century warship. This fact also supports the theory that this was the very picture which Arend Hybertsson might have shown to King Gustaf II Adolf.

However, the engraving indicates 1626 as the year the ship was built, and it can thus not have been the basis of Hybertsson's contract of 1625. Maybe it was shown later, in 1627, when Arend Hybertsson returned from a business journey to Holland, but the *Wasa* was by then at such an advanced stage of construction that the picture could not possibly have influenced the design, and it could definitely not have served as any kind of prototype or pattern for the *Wasa*. In any case it was of no real value as a vindication of the *Wasa* design. Furthermore the engraving is not to scale or in proportion, and differs from the *Wasa* in many vital respects. The ship on the picture has 46 gunports against 70 gunports for the *Wasa*. The upper battery deck is not enclosed like that of the *Wasa*, only built over with transverse beams ("cat-walk").

The purpose of Arend Hybertsson's eloquent arguments about this "prototype" was probably to create some well needed confusion, maybe also to put the blame on the absent King.

Fewer Guns

In the French War Archives in Vincennes there is a preserved inventory for the *Saint Louis*, and a transcript is also preserved in Bibliothéque Nationale in Paris. This list is a good clue to what equipment there was on board the *Wasa*, as the two ships are contemporary and of the same size. (*Saint Louis* and 1 100 tons *Wasa* 1 210 tons.) According to this list the *Saint Louis* had 26—24 pounders and 2—12 pounders, thus a much lighter armament than that of the *Wasa* (planned to carry 60—24 pounders and in reality fitted with "just" 48).

The relationship between the *Wasa* and this "prototype" is thus very vague, and if a comparison is made it also points in the direction that the possible prototype carried a much lighter armament.

Most probably the shipbuilder Henrik Hybertsson had planned the *Wasa* to have just one enclosed battery deck. No Swedish ship before *Wasa* had two complete enclosed gun decks. Possibly the *Äpplet*, commenced in 1619, was an exception in having two decks, but she was repeatedly being rebuilt and was never completed, perhaps as a lesson from the *Wasa* disaster, although the reasons why she remained unifinished are not mentioned in the preserved records. There

was one giant ship built in 1561—63, the *Mars* (or *Makalös* = *Unrivalled*) of 1 780 tons, but even this is not said to have had more than one single enclosed battery deck.

The Responsibility of the Master Shipwright

The shipbuilder Henrik Hybertsson calculated the main dimensions, the form and the proportions, based on the planned length and beam according to the "Dutch School" as he had been taught. His efforts in naval architecture were then devoted to establishing the dimensions of the hull structure and the very complicated manufacturing problems. With the launching of the hull his design responsibility was essentially finished, except for his acting as a manager for the manufacture and mounting of the sculptures, the guncarriages, the rigging and also the future maintenance work. He had hardly any influence on the equipment and the armament. He was hoping, of course, that all would go as well as normal, following the usual routine, and that the completion of the *Wasa* would offer no radical exceptions to common practice.

But he was to be wrong. This time well tried rules were upset. *Wasa* was more and more to take the character of an experimental ship. Many novelties were introduced, all with good intentions, but they all contributed to her loss of stability and to her final disaster.

Armament:
Plans and Changes

As mentioned before there was no drawing, description or specification to go from for the construction, equipment, execution or armament. With regard to the armament the shipbuilder was only expected to arrange the necessary number and size of gun ports in the hull. In volume 9 of *Wasa* studies "Sjöstrid på Wasas tid" ("Naval Fighting in the Time of the *Wasa*"), Anders Sandström has described in detail the armament plans for the *Wasa*. This will be summarized below.

To find out the plans for the armament we must search in the requirement lists of the shipyard and the Ordnance Master. We find the *Wasa* mentioned for the first time in the files for 1627—32 under "List of guns for His Majesty's Fleet 1627". For *"Store Wasan"* is here noted 36—24 pounders, 24—12 pounders, 8—48 pound mortars and 10 small guns for the fighting tops. The mortars were large bore, short guns. They were intended for use at close quarters in preparation for boarding, when the enemy's decks were to be fired at with a swarm of shrapnel. The top guns were light guns placed high up in the masts, intended to engage from above in the deck fighting.

One or Two Gundecks?

Obviously the main armament was too numerous to be accomodated on one enclosed deck and one open deck. This led to the decision that the *Wasa* would have two enclosed battery decks. She was probably the first ship in Sweden to be built in this way.

Information about the Danish ship *Sancta Sophia* could have contributed to the decision. In an article in the Danish journal Tidskrift i Søvaesen in 1960 Commander P Holck suggests that the Swedish Navy decided to build the *Wasa* bigger and more heavily

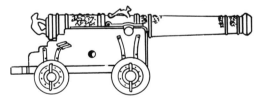

One of the Wasa's guns. Drawing by Eva Marie Stolth.

armed in order that she would match the Danish ship *Sancta Sophia*. This ship was being built in 1624—27, thus in the period when the *Wasa* was planned and begun. She was similar in size, 36.87 m long at the keel and with 10.7 m beam. The *Wasa* is 38.87 ×

The raising of one of the Wasa's 24 pound guns. Three have been found.
The others were raised already in the 17th century.

One of the guns was found on board only after the salvaging of the Wasa.

11.3 m. She had two enclosed battery decks with ports for 50 guns, but in reality she only carried 40—24 pounders, according to "Svenska Flottans Historia" ("History of the Swedish Navy") published by Allhem. Anyway it is quite possible that intelligence reports about the *Sancta Sophia* could have inspired the leading gunnery officers, and perhaps the King himself, to decide on two gun decks and an unusually powerful armament.

However when this decision was

said that he built the *Wasa* one foot, five inches wider than originally planned (on his own responsibility or after consulting his sick boss?). However, as the bottom was already fixed, this could only apply to the

Dutch carpenters at work. Detail from the drawing by van Yk.

made, the hull of the *Wasa* was already under construction. The bottom was already laid, and the beam at the bottom thereby settled. Hein Jacobsson, Hybertsson's assistant,

upper parts from the chine and upwards. The convex frame form at the waterline became still more pronounced, and the contribution to the stability was negligible.

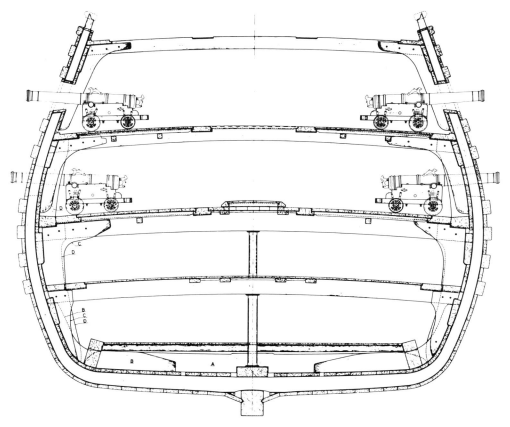

The midship section of the Wasa. Dimensions are heavy, in particular the floor timbers A, bilge knees B and deck beam knees C. The space underneath the floor was meant for ballast, but the space is limited by heavy bilge stringers, floor timbers and bilge knees.

Of course the frames and the skin planking had to be extended upwards because of the extra deck, with its knees, brackets, stiffeners and beams, and all this added to the hull weight.

Reinforcements

The hull structure was given very generous dimensions, certainly in order to support the increased weight of the guns. The heavy longitudinal girders along the chine are for instance a type of reinforcement, which only much later in the 17th century came into general use.

Some strakes of the skin planking were usually given double thickness in order to protect the skin planking and to compensate for the loss of strength at the gunport openings. The *Wasa* was fitted with no less than six such thicker strakes, four below and two above the lower gun ports.

It was usual to let the frame parts overlap each other for a distance where the parts were joined. Due to the heavy frame dimensions and their small spacing the result was that the framing became "full-timbered" along the enclosed battery, which helped to prevent gunballs breaking through the hull. However, the *Wasa* differs from the scheme in having most spaces between the frames full-timbered and filled with beams and logs.

Quite possibly, the *Wasa* became the first Swedish warship with a proper oven made of bricks. Zettersten mentions in his "Svenska Flottans historia" ("History of the Swedish Navy") that the use of a heavy brick oven on board the ships in 1660 was still a novelty.

Unitary Armament

However, in the Shipyard Requirement List the line "30—24 pounders" has later been crossed out and replaced by "60—24 pounders", while all 12- and 6 pounders were omitted. The alteration is not dated. Now a unitary armament had obviously been decided on, which meant that also the upper battery deck was to have 24 pounders. From a gunnery point of view, a unitary armament had much to commend itself. The ammunition store on board could be better utilized with just one size of gun. Carriages and all accessories could be

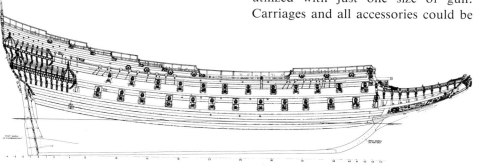

More Weight Additions

But there were still more weight additions to come: If we look at the "Proposals for His Royal Majesty's Fleet of 1628" the armament plan for the *Wasa* was altered to 30—24 pounders, 30—12 pounders, 8—6 pounders, 4—48 pound mortars and 2—24 pound mortars. It had obviously become apparent that the lower deck could only have 30 gunports, and consequently the number of 24-pounders was reduced from 36 to 30. On the other hand the number of 12-pounders was correspondingly increased, and 8—6-pounders added.

rationalized. The *Wasa* was to become the first "all-big-gun" capital ship, a forerunner of HMS *Dreadnought* from 1906. It is also well known that King Gustaf II Adolf was very interested in gunnery and a strong advocate of standardising to a few types and sizes.

The hull was by then finished up to the upper deck, for the upper gunports are in fact smaller than those on the lower deck, as they were originally intended for 12 pounders only.

The upper gunports and the whole upper battery deck could no longer be changed, so Hein Jacobsson could only hope that the deck and its beams would stand up to the weight of the 24 pounders.

In fact the plan for 60—24 pound guns was unrealistic. The two enclosed gundecks had just 54 broadside ports plus two rear facing ports on the lower deck. This explains why we find another two figures for the Wasa armament in the Shipyard Requirement Plans for 1628: The first says 54—24 pounders, 12—12 pounders and 4 mortars, the second 58—24 pounders, 8—12 pounders and 6 mortars. In the first case all the 12 pounders would have to be placed on the upper, open deck, in the second even eight of the heavy 24 pounders would have had to be placed on the upper deck.

Armament Decided by Supply

In reality the number of guns was determined by the production, which was delayed. The difficulties are also illustrated by the fact that the recovered guns are found to be of rather imprecise quality, cast without proper alignment and finish, typical signs of great haste. On the basis of the number and the position of the guncarriages actually found, Commodore Clason has calculated the number of guns on board *Wasa* when she sailed. His calculations give a total of 56 guns of which 48 were 24 pounders, 24 on each of the two enclosed battery decks. The two carriages behind the rear facing transom ports had not received any guns. Their bearing caps were still bolted in position. The early recovery of most of the guns had started with unscrewing the bearing caps by aid of tools introduced through the ports, a phenomenal achievement with the means and resources of those days.

In 1664—1665, Hans Albrecht von Treileben and his divers succeeded in raising most of the Wasa's guns, using a diving bell.

The Stability Test

While the *Wasa* was still being fitted out at the quay outside the Royal Castle, she was found to be unstable. This was proven during a stability test carried out in the presence of Admiral Fleming. However, it is remarkable that neither of the two shipbuilders, Hein Jacobsson or Johan Isbrandsson, who were interrogated by the Court of Inquiry, was present at the test or were informed about its alarming outcome. After this far from convincing stability test it is also surprising that both Admiral Fleming and the Captain, Söfring Hansson, who were experienced naval officers, agreed to let the *Wasa* set out on her expedition. The explanation was of course the great urgency to get her commissioned. She was already delayed and the King had in writing ordered that "both the *Wasa* and the *Kronan* shall be ready by the next Jacobi, (that is 25th July), and if not, those responsible would be subject to His Majestys disgrace".

The Test was Stopped

After the disaster it was natural that both Admiral Fleming and Captain Söfring Hansson were deeply worried that the inquiry would reveal their excessive optimism in ignoring the result of the stability test. Neither of them said anything about the test in their testimony. It was in fact the rather outspoken boatswain Matsson who revealed that a stability test had been made. He told the Court that Söfring Hanson had said to the Admiral that the ship was unstable, and that they had ordered 30 men to run from one side of the ship to the other. "The first time", said boatswain Matsson, "it heeled over by one plank, the second time two planks and the third time three planks". Then, he said, the Admiral had ordered the testing to be stopped and had said that "if they had run over the ship one more time she would have capsized". The Admiral had also uttered a wish "that His Royal Majesty had been at home".

"God Grant..."

The boatswain Matsson also claimed to have said to the Admiral that "the ship was narrow at the bottom and lacked enough belly". He said that the Admiral had answered that "you carry too much ballast so that the cannon-ports come too close to the water". Matsson then claimed to have answered by praying to higher powers "God, grant that the ship will stand upright on her keel". The Admiral had then consoled him by saying that "the shipbuilder has built ships before

"God grant that the ship will stand upright on her keel", said boatswain Matsson after the stability test had been stopped. Thirty men had been running back and forth across the deck of the Wasa. After three times, Admiral Fleming stopped the test. Otherwise, the ship would have capsized by the quay. Drawing by Ann Forslind.

and he should not be worried". So the Admiral put his faith in his authorities, the deceased shipbuilder Henrik Hybertsson and his successor Hein Jacobsson, while boatswain Matsson had to put his faith in Our Lord.

It is possible to calculate the metacentric height and the initial stiffness from a correctly executed stability test. However, in the case of the *Wasa*, the measuring methods were very primitive and thus the results have a high degree of uncertainty. It is for instance unclear to what extent the equipment had been taken on board. Judging from the inquiry records all the ballast was taken on board except for one boat-load. But how much was one boat-load? The armament was probably only partly on board, for it is known that this fitting out work was going on until the 31st July.

The heeling angle is given as a certain number of "planks". Does this refer to the breadth of *Wasas* actual skin planks? Or was one "plank" a generally accepted measure?

Another factor of uncertainty is that the witness, boatswain Matsson, did not personally take part in the test. He was merely a worried spectator. It is quite possible that Admiral Klas Fleming and Captain Söfring Hansson did know a lot more about the stability test and its result, but they were wise enough to keep silent about it.

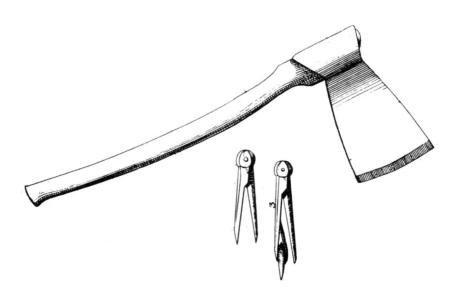

What is Stability?

A ship floating in water takes such a position that the weight of the displaced water equals the weight of the ship, *Archimedes' law*. To be in equilibrium the ship assumes such a position that its *centre of gravity* and *centre of the displacement volume* are right above each other. The gravity force and the upthrust of the displacement (the buoyancy force) are equal and opposed when the body is at rest.

For a ship the centre of gravity is usually situated above the center of buoyancy. Thus the situation would seem to be instable, but it is in fact stable as the hull returns to its upright position as soon as the hull is heeled over a small angle.

We can assume that no loose weights are moved and that the centre of gravity remains in the same position.

Form Stability

When heeling the ship, the displacement takes another form. Its centre will move and the buoyancy force attacks at a new point. If the ship has got *form stability*, the centre of displacement moves in such a direction that the gravity force and the buoyancy force constitute a righting couple. The couple can be represented by the length of the lever arm between the two forces. This lever arm can be plotted over the angle of heel. Such a graph is called the *curve of static stability*, and illustrates the stiffness and stability characteristics of the ship. For a normal ship the curve will first rise to a maximum and then fall off. The point, where the lever arm reaches zero corresponds to the angle of heel where the ship capsizes.

Let us first return to the zero angle

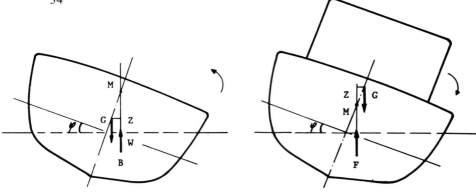

The gravity force attacks at the centre of gravity G. The buoyancy force attacks at the centre of the displacement. Together they constitute a couple which acts in a righting direction (left figure) or a heeling direction (right figure).

The metacentre M is the intersection of the centreline and the line of the buoyancy force.

The metacentric height is the distance GM between the centre of gravity G and the metacentre M. As long as GM has a positive value (metacentre above centre of gravity) the couple is righting. If GM becomse negative the couple is heeling and the ship can not take an upright position.

and heel the hull an infinitely small angle. The line of the buoyancy force will in this case intersect the centre line of the ship at the *metacentre*. The distance from the metacentre to the centre of gravity is the *metacentric height*. The higher up the centre of gravity, the smaller is the metacentric height and the weaker the ship. However, a high metacentric height is not in itself an essential or necessary criterion for a good stability. A low metacentric height can well be acceptable, provided the centre of buoyancy moves sufficiently to the heeled side of the ship as the heel increases.

The metacentric height is just an expression for the initial stiffness of the hull and can only illustrate the initial stability.

Weight Stability

There are some special cases where the centre of gravity is situated lower than the centre of buoyancy. Such is the case with most submarines and sailing yachts with a heavy keel. When such a ship is heeled over, the centre of buoyancy must not neccessarily be moved athwartships so as to create a form stability. Such a ship is said to possess *weight stability* and can not capsize as long as all weights on board remain in place and the hull stays watertight.

The purpose of the righting couple, which hopefully is created by a heel, is to counteract the external heeling forces which the ship is subjected to. For a sailing ship these come mainly from the wind pressure on the sails. We know that the *Wasa* capsized for a squall.

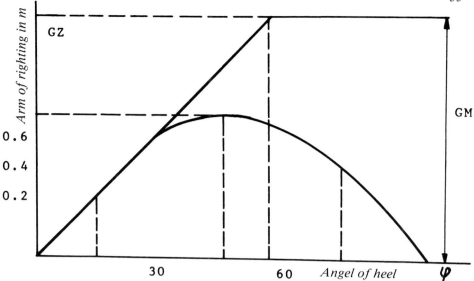

The curve of static stability shows how the righting moment varies with increasing angle of heel. The figure shows a normal conditon, where the arm of righting moment increases up to a certain maximum value, whereupon it falls to zero at an angle where the ship will capsize without any outside heeling moment at all.

A heeling wind force is largest at 0° and will decrease with increasing angle of heel. The wind force is counteracted by the righting forces. A balance is attained at a certain angle of heel. If the lever-arm of the righting couple is reduced, this angle of balance is reached at an increasingly higher angle, until the wind force can no longer be counteracted, and the ship will capsize.

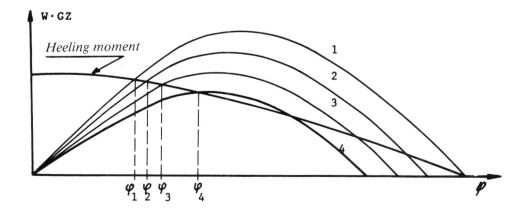

We do not know the wind force, but obviously it can not have been any worse than what a newbuilt and intact warship was expected to stand up to.

With a sudden squall an additional problem comes into the picture: It will cause the ship to rotate around its length axis and will feed rotational energy into the ship. The result is, as with a flywheel, that the heeling movement will continue even when the sudden squall is over. Thus, when we study the *Wasa's* stability curve and its ability to withstand the forces from a squall it is not enough just to consider the static stability. It must also be taken into account that the process is a dynamic one.

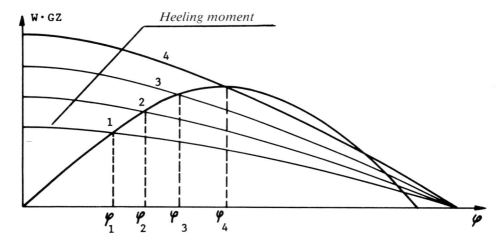

If a ship with a certain curve of static stability is subjected to an increased heeling wind force the intersection of the curves will move towards larger angles of heel. Finally the heeling couple will surmount the righting couple and the ship will capsize.

On the opposite side: Body plan for the Wasa. Drawn from measurings.

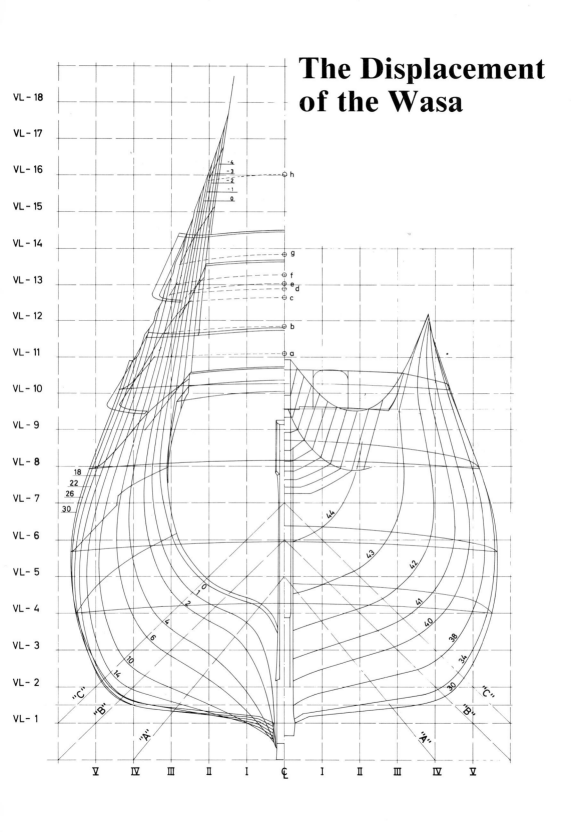

The Displacement of the Wasa

38

What was the displacement of the *Wasa*? It was equal to the weight, but no weight calculation or even estimation was ever made during the planning or building. Now it can be done and has been done, but due to lack of knowledge about much of the rigging and equipment the result is still very imprecise. We could get some idea about the displacement if we knew her draught in the water.

The Inspector of Ordnance Erik Jönsson said during the inquiry that the lower gunports were 3 1/2 feet from the water. Lieutenant Petter Gierdsson, who had been supervising the rigging work, said, however, that the gunports were 4—4 1/2 feet from the water and that she drew 14 feet forward and 16 feet aft and 15 feet midships.

answers that he is a gunnery officer, not an Admiral or a Captain, and that he is no expert on ballasting. But the interrogator then replies that the shipbuilder (Hein Jacobsson?) had said that if he had been informed that the ship was unstable, then he (the shipbuilder) would have seen to it that she had been loaded down (with ballast) one foot deeper. To this Erik Jönsson replies that it would not have been possible, as the gun ports were already only 3 1/2 feet from the water. In order to support his opinion that there was already enough ballast, Erik Jönsson must have had an interest in under-estimating the available freeboard.

The Captain's signature — Söfring Hansson.

His testimony is probably more reliable than Erik Jönsson's. The latter was pressed hard by the interrogator, Admiral Karl Karlsson Gyllenhielm, who accused Erik Jönsson of not having seen to it that the ship was correctly ballasted. It appears from the record that Erik Jönsson was feeling offended by this accusation. He

Displacement 1,210 Cubic Metres
On the other hand it seems probable that Lieutenant Petter Gierdsson had actually checked and read the depth figures fore and aft. These depth marks and figures are still there and are still fully readable on the hull. Consequently there is no need to speculate about whether it is Dutch or

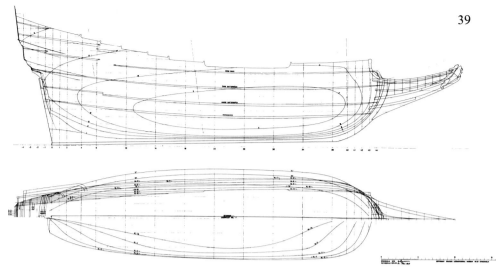

Swedish feet or about the length of a foot.

We only need to mark the draft 14 feet forward and 16 feet aft on the linear drawing and draw a line between them to arrive at the real waterline. The displacement below this waterline has been calculated as 1,210 m³. The medium draft from the keelline to the waterline is found to be 4.8 m. From this the displacement centre can also be calculated with the normal geometric methods of naval architecture.

The Wasa departs on the 10th of August 1628. Water colour by Nils Stödberg.

The Form Stability of the Wasa

Since the *Wasa* was raised her hull has been carefully measured. Based on this a linear drawing has been made up. The stability figures have been calculated by aid of a computer. The stability curves have been drawn up, first separately without regard to the centre of gravity (c.o.g), the so called pantocarenes, later with certain assumed positions of the c.o.g. One is struck by the flatness of these curves as compared with the curves for normal, modern ships and boats. This means in practice that even a very high value of the metacentric height will not bring the lever arm curve up to the desired value at larger angles of heel. In other words, the form stability of the *Wasa* does not increase sufficiently as the angles of heel increase.

Geometrically this is dictated by the shape of the frames. According to the "Dutch School" the master frame or midship section is composed of a number of straight lines and circles. At the waterline the frames are convex with the form of a circle. Above the water-line the sides are sloping inwards with a

In the Beckholmen dry dock after the salvage. Although severely damaged, the stern is still an impressive sight.

pronounced "tumble home". Such a form was common for contemporary warships, the purpose being to improve the fighting conditions during a boarding. In the *Wasa*, convex form at the waterline has become still more pronounced because Hein Jacobsson, the shipbuilder, had increased the beam by one foot, five inches, but only above the chine. He did so probably since he became aware that the ship was to get two complete enclosed gun decks and a heavier armament than usual. Intuitively, he has tried to make the hull stiffer by widening it. Similar methods of increasing the initial stiffness were not so uncommon for existing ships when they were found to be too tender. The breadth was then increased at the waterline by nailing another layer of skin planks to the skin. The process was called "girdling". However, even if this improved the initial stiffness its effect on the stability at larger angles of heel was almost nil.

Minimal Form Stability

The situation can also be expressed by saying that most 17th century warships had a very low form stability. This was probably still more so for ships designed to the English than to the Dutch School of the art. Sometimes, one has reason to doubt whether

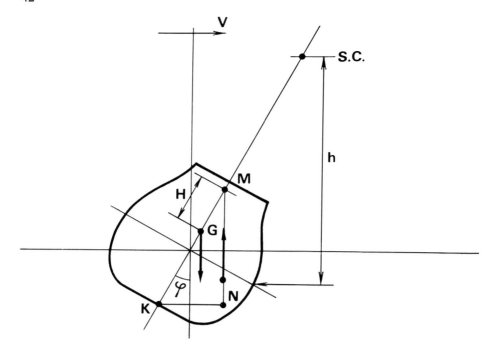

v =   *wind velocity* = *4 m/s* = *8 knots*
C_P =   *wind pressure coefficient* = *1*
A =   *sail area* = *601 m²*
S.C. =   *sail centre*
Sc =   *air density* = *1.27 kg/m³*
Sv =   *water density* = *1005 kg/m³*
h =   *lever arm from sail centre to centre of water pressure*
V =   *displacement volume* = *1210 m³*
g =   *gravity coefficient* = *9.81 m/s²*
GZ =   *lever arm*
G =   *centre of gravity*
M =   *metacentre*
K =   *baseline*
φ =   *angle of heel*

The heeling moment from the wind pressure on the sails is $M_S = \dfrac{Av^2}{2} \cdot S_l \cdot h \cdot C_p$

The righting moment from the static stability is $M_v = V_{S_v} \cdot g \cdot GZ$

If the two moments balance each other, $M_v = M_S$ *we can calculate the lever arm of the static stability as*

$$GZ = \frac{Av^2 Sl \cdot h \cdot Cp}{2 \cdot V \cdot g \cdot Sv}$$

KM is found to be 6.3 m according to the pantocarenes
K—S.C. is measured to be = 26.25 m

The transverse water pressure on the lateral plane is assumed to have its centre at half draft, thus at 4.8/2 = 2.4 m below the waterline.

For small angles of heel the lever arm h is calculated at h = 26.25—2.4 = 23.85 m and GZ can be calculated to

$$GZ = \frac{601 \cdot 4^2 \cdot 1.27 \cdot 23.85 \cdot 1}{2 \cdot 1210 \cdot 1005 \cdot 9.81} = 0.012\ m$$

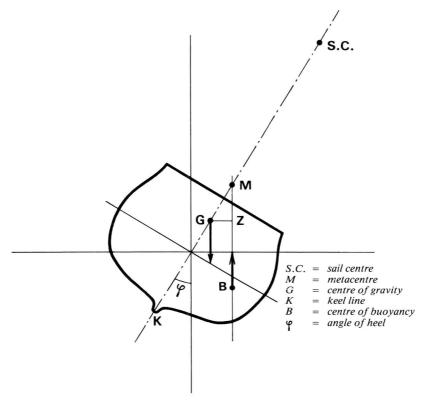

S.C. = sail centre
M   = metacentre
G   = centre of gravity
K   = keel line
B   = centre of buoyancy
φ   = angle of heel

the ships had any form stability whatsoever. The reason why the ships normally did not capsize was that this lack of form stability was compensated by a substantial weight stability, achieved by proper and liberal ballasting. To ensure this the hull must be sufficiently deep in the hold to accomodate the ballast and bring it down low enough. Another requirement was that the weight of the hull, armament, rigging and equipment in relation to the underwater volume was such as to allow sufficient margin for the necessary ballast weight to be carried.

Minimal Weight Stability

The British ships had rather deep hulls with plenty of space for ballast, so the first requirement was easily met. The Dutch ships were often more problematic with their flatbottomed hulls, which were more suited to the shallow waters along the Dutch coast. The *Wasa* hardly complied with any of the above requirements. Like all Dutch designs she was rather flatbottomed and had a rather limited space for the ballast. She was also so heavily built and armed that the available weight margin for the ballast was clearly insufficient to give her the well needed weight stability.

Most 17th century warships had such a low form stability that they were entirely dependent on weight stability by ballasting. As a result they were very sensitive to the position of the c.o.g. Even a small change in the c.o.g. would completely change their stability characteristics.

The Wind Pressure
on the Sails

Calculation of the c.o.g. from weight estimations will have to be based on many uncertain factors. It is therefore worth while to try to approach the problem from another angle. We know that the *Wasa* did capsize in a light squall. We can start out from this and investigate what forces were acting on her at the moment she capsized.

We know that there was very little wind. Captain Söfring Hansson says the day after the disaster that "there came a squall". Lieutenant Petter Gierdsson said during the main inquiry: "The weather was not strong enough to pull out the sheets, although the blocks were well lubricated. Therefore they had to push the sheets out, and one man was enough to hold the sheet". From this it would seem that an

Reconstruction of the rig of the Wasa. Drawing by Eva-Marie Stolth.

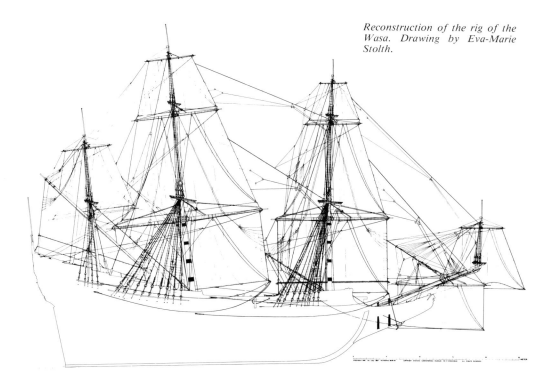

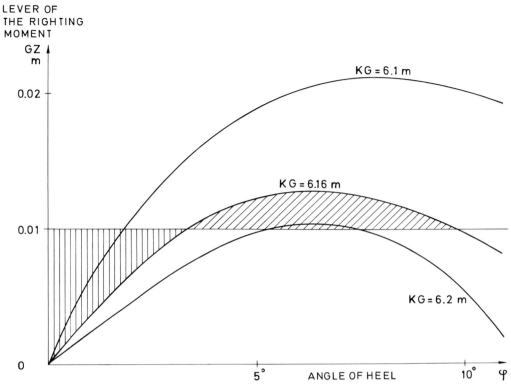

LEVER OF
THE RIGHTING
MOMENT

represents the inertia absorbed by the ship while the heeling moment is greater than the rightling moment

represents the "braking" inertia returned by the ship while the righting moment is greater than the heeling moment. In the example with centre of gravity 6.16 m above the heel the two areas become equal at 10°. Thus, the ship will continue to heel over more than 10° and finally capsize.

For an assumed value of KG = 6.16 m we get the following table:

φ	KN	sin φ	KG sin φ	GZ
5°	0.55	0.0872	0.54	0.01
10°	1.08	0.1736	1.07	0.01
20°	1.98	0.3420	2.11	-0.13

From this table it is clear that the GZ-value is too low to prevent the ship from capsizing even for such a low wind velocity as 4 m/s. To sum up the basic figures which are of importance for explaining the capsizing are:

Metacentre position above baseline KM = 6.3 m
Centre of gravity above baseline KG = 6.16 m
Metacentrie height KM—KG = 6.3—6.16 = 0.14 m

assumed wind velocity of eight knots in the squall would not be too far from the truth. Petter Gierdsson also indicates which sails were set, both topsails, the foresail and the mizzen. Most parts of the rigging have been recovered. From this, the sail area has been calculated to 601 m².

The position of the sail centre has been calculated to 26.25 m from the keel-line. The coefficient for the wind pressure can be assumed to be = 1.

From the stability curves the meta-centre is found to be situated 6.3 m above the keel-line at a displacement of 1,210 m³ and a draft of 4.8 m. From the above figures the righting lever arm is found to be 0.0102 m when the two couples balance each other.

Thus if the heeling process had been slow, so that static conditions hade prevailed, and if the righting lever arm had been 0.0102 m, the *Wasa* would have capsized for a wind velocity of eight knots. This is the case with a c.o.g. 6.2 m above the baseline of the linear drawing.

Metacentric Height
14 Centimetres

However, as underlined above, the process was probably quick and of dynamic nature. The inertia force caused by the dynamic energy fed into the moving system by the sudden squall must be added to the heeling force from the wind. When this is also taken into account it is found that with a c.o.g. 6.16 m above the base-line the ship will capsize when the list reaches 10°. The metacentric height would then have been 6.3 m minus 6.16, that is 0.14 m, a far too low value. It is hard to say what

was a "normal" metacentric height for a ship like the *Wasa*, but as a comparison for sailing ships from the last turn of century metacentric heights of about 0.5—1.0 m have been quoted.

The graph has also tentatively been completed with a lever-arm curve for an assumed c.o.g. 6.1 m above the base-line. This curve illustrates that even this slight lowering of the c.o.g. by 6 cm would have improved the *Wasa's* stiffness enough to withstand the assumed squall of eight knots. This does not mean that it would have cured the trouble and turned the *Wasa* into a seaworthy ship, but it proves how sensitive a hull of this form is to small changes in the c.o.g.

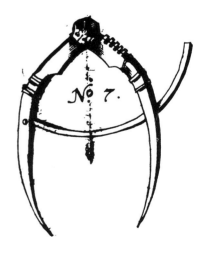

The Wasa's Centre of Gravity (c.o.g.)

It has been shown in the previous chapters that the *Wasa*, like most contemporary warships, had a very low form stability. It would have been lower still if she had been designed according to the British instead of the Dutch School. But she would have had a deeper hull with more room for ballast.

"Heavier Above than Below"

The records from the inquiries held after the accident give the impression that most of the people involved had an intuitive feeling that there must have been something wrong with the weight or the ballasting. But what was wrong? The whole stability problem was a most

Ship carpenters at work. From "Skeppsbyggeri" ("On Shipbuilding") by Rålamb, 1691.

Whether such a ship comes out stiff or weak is entirely dependent on the position of the c.o.g. The difference between success and failure can be a question of a few centimetres.

obscure one, and everyone had difficulties in expressing themselves in a clear way. For instance the Inspector of Ordnance Erik Jönsson said that he is no expert on ballasting but that "the ship was heavier above than below". The Judge asks the shipbuilder Johan Isbrandsson "why the superstructure was heavier than the lower part".

During the analysis attempted after the inquiries one of those present says; "in order that the keel should have been able to carry the weight above the water there should have been more weight below". Another says: "The ship is heavier above than below..." Captain Clerck says: "... the hold should have been 2 feet deeper so that more ballast could have been put in ..." Lasse Bubz says: "The superstructure was heavier than the lower part." Master Wellam says: "... therefore it is heavier above than below ..." Hans Förrådz: "... the ship was too sharply built below so that it could not carry the superstructure ..."

Most of the experts agreed that the ship was topheavy but no one understood the real mechanism. Words like "centre of gravity" or "stability" did not exist in the language. Nor could anyone go a step further and ask why and in what way the ship had become topheavy. The weight of the hull, the equipment and the guns are never mentioned. The guns are only mentioned in connection with the doubt that they might not have been properly secured and come adrift. To add to the confusion most people had the general feeling that the higher and more impressive a warship looked and the more and bigger guns it carried, the more indestructible would it also be. The shipbuilders, Arend Hybertsson, Hein Jacobsson and Johan Isbrandsson expressed their great pride in their product, which they say "is well and

The arms of the Krämer family from 1662.

sturdily built", and to his part of the quality we can certainly agree.

"God Alone Can Know"

In spite of all efforts to find a scapegoat and to clarify the real cause of the

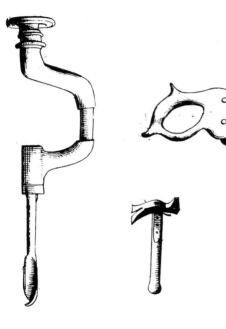

disaster the Court at last found themselves faced with a riddle, which could not be solved by any human efforts. At the end of the inquiry the Judge asked the witnesses outright how the ship could have capsized although she was correctly built. They then answered according to the records, that "they can not know, God alone can know this". In any case nobody was declared guilty, and nobody was officially reprimanded or punished. That such a costly and beautiful ship could so suddenly capsize and sink in practically calm weather must have been felt as such a shock that it had

to be attributed to some supernatural and almighty power.

Today it would be possible in theory to calculate all the weights, to measure all the hull components and sum up the hull weight. We have to assume density figures of the wood (which differ between various parts) and also add the weights of all masts, spars, beams, sails, guns and equipment. This would also permit calculation of the c.o.g. However there are so many uncertain factors and rough estimations to be accounted for that it is doubtful if such a work is worth while.

Most probably the method of calculating "backwards" from the balance of forces which we know led to the accident gives a much better indication of the real c.o.g.

By this method the c.o.g. is found to have been situated 6.16 m above the baseline. It is also evident from the calculations that if the c.o.g. of the *Wasa* had been only about 5—10 cm lower she would at least not have capsized in the harbour.

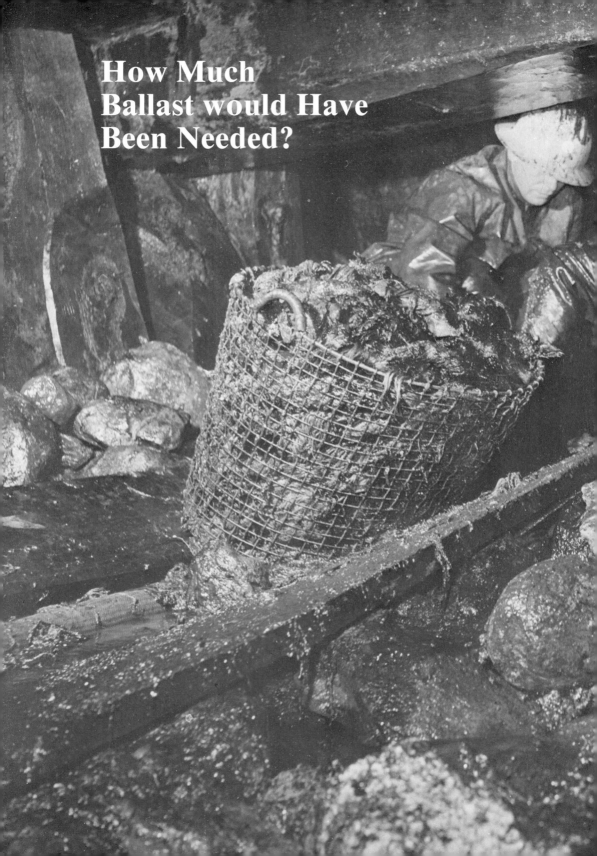

How Much
Ballast would Have
Been Needed?

The stability of the *Wasa* was entirely dependent on the position of the c.o.g. and this in turn was strongly influenced by the amount and position of the ballast. In fact the discussions during the main inquiry also came to circle around the question of ballast.

The experts and the witnesses all seem to have had the intuitive feeling that the ballast was at fault, but there were divided opinions as to *what* was the fault with the ballast. Some had wanted more ballast, other less ballast. Admiral Klas Fleming, who of course was very influential, had wanted *less ballast*. Captain Söfring Hansson, when he was interrogated the day after the accident, said that there was one hundred lasts more of ballast than Admiral Fleming had wanted. This coincides with the testimony of the boatswain, Matsson, who claims that the Admiral had accused him of carrying too much ballast when he had complained to the Admiral that the ship seemed "too narrow in the bottom". Admiral Fleming had answered: "You are carrying too much ballast; the gunports are too close to the water!" This must have confused poor Matsson as he on the contrary "had put in as much ballast as there was room for".

The judge said to Erik Jönsson that the shipbuilder (Hein Jacobsson) had

said that "had he been informed that the ship was unstable, and if he had been ordered to, he would have seen to it that it hade been loaded down one foot deeper". Thus, in his opinion she should have had *more ballast*.

Little Influence for the Master Shipwright

This statement immediately illuminates the cardinal problem: the lack of coordination and the remarkably little influence the shipbuilder had on the total project. He says he was not even

told that the ship was unstable! And only if he had been ordered (by whom?) he would have seen to it that more ballast had been put in. Maybe Admiral Fleming and Erik Jönsson intuitively and intentionally avoided to notify him as they feared that he would suggest more ballasting which would have brought the gun ports lower and thus restrict the use of the guns.

However, even if there were divided

Preceding page: The ballast stones in the hold of the Wasa did not leave much room for the archaeologists.

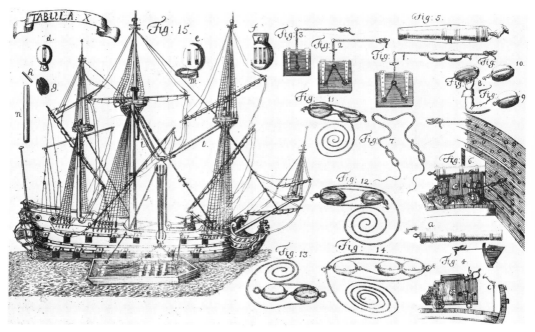

The artillery is brought on board. From "Skeppsbyggeri" ("On Shipbuilding") by Rålamb 1691. The weight of the Wasa's guns was carefully documented, while the cobblestone ballasting was done by rough estimate.

opinions among the witnesses, most of the Court members seem to have instinctively felt that more ballast should have been taken in. Says Captain Clerck: "... would the hold have been 2 feet deeper, so that more ballast could have been put in, then it would have stood upright". Master Wellam: "'... that the load in the bottom was too light.." and "'... the ballast is lying too high, and there are the big beams which take up the room for the ballast."

Ballasting by Feeling

In reality the ballasting was done just "by feeling". No one knew what weight was needed, and no weights were checked. The amount was mainly governed by *the available space*. The stone ballast could not be placed directly on the bottom planking, for this space was completely filled by the closely spaced bottom frames and the fillets between them. On top of this came the inner planking and on top of this the transverse bottom beams. Athwartships the space was limited by the stout chine girders.

Boatswain Matsson seems to have been aware that there was very little room for the ballast, for he said during the inquiry that he did not quite trust that his men and the crew could stow the ballast properly, so "he went himself below with a light and stowed as much as he could". Maybe they could have got in some more if they had lifted the bottom floor a bit. But its position was determined by the top of the chine girders. To modify this would have meant a major step which boatswain Matsson could certainly not have undertaken on his own. And no other person in a leading position had been below and seen what it looked like. Matsson probably emerged from the hold, reporting that "now it's filled up down there", and everybody was satisfied.

More Ballast Possible

Another limitation was *the height of the gunports* above the water. Erik Jönsson says this was 3 1/2 feet, Petter Gierdsson 4—4 1/2 feet, but it was probably never measured. If we now measure from the waterline we arrive at from Petter Gierdssons draft figures, 14 feet forward and 16 feet aft, we find the height of the lowest gunport to be 4.8 feet. So both witnesses erred on the low side.

How high above the waterline were normally placed the lower edges of the gunports at that time? We know that later on, the gundecks were usually positioned higher (which was made possible by increased weight stability)

in order to allow the artillery to be used at a greater degree of heel and in hard weather. In the case of the *Wasa*, a somewhat larger quantity of ballast and, consequently, a lower freeboard would probably have been acceptable. But no one proposed this, as all available space was said to be filled. The only person who could have insisted, Master Shipwright Hein Jacobsson, said that he had not even been told that the ship was unstable!

An Insoluble Problem

Such additional ballast, within the limit set by the required altitude of the gunports above the water, might have saved the *Wasa* from capsizing in a light gust of wind in the harbour. She would, however, still have been a "crank" ship, and the disaster would probably only have been postponed. With the weights present on board and their distribution, the stability problem was in fact insoluble.

The Distribution of the Ballast

After the *Wasa* had been raised and docked, the cobblestone ballast was

unloaded in the summer of 1961. The volumes were measured and the ballast was weighed. Sam Svensson, then a Curator at the Maritime Museum, in a report divides the ballast into three groups:

One group of 5.35 tons with an estimated volume of 2.5 m³ was located close the bilge pump, between frames 6 and 10.

One group of 8.49 tons with an estimated volume of 4.3 m³ was located in the area near the foremast and the bitts, between frames 36 and 40.

The main part of the ballast was under the loose floor in the area from the frame space immediately ahead of the stern hatch to a space ahead of the fore hatch, i.e. between frames 11 and 36. This group weighed 105.14 tons. In addition, there was an estimated 2—3 tons of pebbles left in the emptied spaces. The volume of the spaces is given as 84.42 m³.

The real weight of the ballast was thus 121—122 tons. The weight per volume for the first two groups is 2.14 and 1.97 tons per m³, respectively, while the weight/volume of the main quantity is only 1.27 tons per m³. This indicates that the ballast was not as well stowed as boatswain Matsson and Captain Hansson maintained during the inquiry. In actual fact, however, this was difficult for them to assess. The hold under the floor was cramped and dark. The men who stowed and inspected the ballast had to crawl and grope their way through the dark in the flickering light of primitive torches.

Another 130 Tons Required

Possibly an additional 70 tons could have been stowed, albeit with a great effort. The centre of gravity of the additional ballast can be estimated at 1.5 m above the keel line, that is 4.66 m below the actual probable centre of gravity. This would, however, have resulted in lowering the centre of gravity by only appx. $\frac{70}{1210}$ x 466 = 2.65 cm. This would not be sufficient to give the Wasa an adequate stability.

In order to give the Wasa a tolerable stability, her centre of gravity would have had to be lowered by at least 5 cm. This would have required an additional 130 tons of ballast, more than double the actual amount. In that case, the Wasa would have been 0.35 m deeper in the water and the distance from the water level to the gunports would have been 3.65 feet (1.11 m) instead of 4.8 feet (1.46 m). In reality, this might have been acceptable, but the responsible authorities, Admiral Fleming and Inspector of Ordnance Erik Jönsson, would certainly have opposed such a proposal. Anyway, there would not have been room for the extra ballast under the floors in the hold. Thus, the problem could not have been solved in this way. The only possibility would have been to reduce the top weight considerably.

In the cramped darkness of the hold of the Wasa, it must have been extremely difficult to judge whether there was room for more ballast. The weight of the stone ballast was 120 tons. Possibly, an additional 70 tons could have been stowed, but this would still not have been sufficient to prevent the disaster.

Why the Wasa Capsized

- [ ] The *Wasa* was probably laid down as a "small" ship and completed as a "large" ship.

- [ ] The building was delayed and the *Wasa* was in the end fulfilled with a great haste.

- [ ] According to earlier plans, the *Wasa* was to be built with *one* enclosed gundeck. Due to circumstances, she was in the end built with *two*.

- [ ] The *Wasa* became an experimental ship, aiming at a maximum of armament without regard to other considerations such as floatability, stability, stiffness and sailing characteristics.

- [ ] Henrik Hybertsson became seriously ill and died a year before the *Wasa* was completed. During his illness he had to delegate the supervision of the project to his assistant, Hein Jacobsson. As a result the leadership on the shipbuilding side was very weak.

- [ ] The armament plan was changed several times during the time of building. From the beginning the first plan specified an armament heavier than the hull could carry and more than could be accomodated on one enclosed battery deck. Gun manufacture was a bottleneck: only 48 of the 24-pounders were completed and brought on board, but their weight was still too high.

- [ ] The hull structure of the *Wasa* was of exceptionally generous dimensions. She had big and heavy longitudinal girders at the chine and the space between the frames was almost filled with reinforcements. As a result the hull plus the armament was heavier than what was until then common practice.

☐ No methods for calculation of stability were known.

☐ No methods of controlling the weight were practiced. The guns were in fact the only equipment where the weight was given, but this was for other reasons and their weight figures were never considered for any shipbuilding calculations.

☐ During fitting out the *Wasa* was ballasted according to common practice. However, the ballast quantity was limited by the small space available (as the heavy frames and girders took up much space in the bottom part) and by the risk that the lower gun ports would come dangerously close to the water. The total weight of the ballast was 121—122 tons. About twice this amount would have been needed to ensure a reasonable stability, but that much could not have been accommodated under the loose floors in the hold and would have brought the gun ports too close to the water.

☐ A stability test was carried out in Admiral Fleming's presence during fitting out. This indicated that the *Wasa* was too weak and unstable. In spite of this, the *Wasa* was commissioned and allowed to sail. The reason for this was surely shortage of time (she was already delayed, and the King had put great pressure on all responsible for her quick completion). Another reason for this was that nobody seemed able to suggest any way of curing the lack of stiffness.

☐ There was no coordination between those responsible for the building of the hull, the decoration, the rigging, the ballasting, and the armament.

☐ When the *Wasa* sailed, her centre of gravity was probably about 6.16 m above the keelline and her metacentric height was about 0.14 m. A sudden squall of eight knots' strength was sufficient to make her capsize. Had the centre of gravity been 5—10 cm lower she would not have capsized in the harbour. This would however have required twice the amount of ballast, which could not have been accommodated, and if so the gun ports would have come too close to the water.

References

Cederlund, Carl Olof, Stockholms skeppsgård och regalskeppet Wasa, S:t Eriks årsbok 1965.

Clason, Edward, Om Wasas bestyckning, Tidskrift i Sjöväsendet 1964.

Franzén, Anders, The warship Vasa, Stockholm 1974.

Hafström, Georg, En bok om skeppet Wasa, Stockholm 1959.

Några problem kring skeppet Wasa, Forum Navale 1963:18, s 17—42.

Utblickar kring tillkomsten av skeppet Wasa, Statens Sjöhistoriska Museum, Meddelande XI, 1968.

Örlogsskeppet Wasas undergång 1628, Tidskrift i Sjöväsendet 1958.

Hammar, Magnus, Historiskt och tekniskt kring Regalskeppet Wasa, Tidskrift i Sjöväsendet 1960.

Janhem, Åke, Varför kantrade skeppet Wasa, Till Rors 1957:4, s 16—17.

Johansen, Ulrich, Hvorfor kaentrede Wasa, Ingeniøren 1962:20.

Mattsson, Einar, Bronskanoner från örlogsskeppen Riksnyckeln och Wasa, Sjöhistorisk Årsbok 1957/58.

Ohrelius, Bengt, Wasa, kungens skepp, Stockholm 1959.

Riksrådets protokoll 1628, Riksarkivet.

Sandström, Anders, Sjöstrid på Wasas tid, Wasastudier nr 9, Stockholm 1982.

Schoerner, Gunnar, Regalskeppet, Stockholm 1964.

Svenska Flottans Historia 1:2, Stockholm 1945.

Svensson, Sam, Wasa och hennes stabilitet, Svensk Sjöfartstidning 1962:46.

Wasas segel och något om äldre segelmakeri, Sjöhistorisk Årsbok 1963/64.

Zettersten, Axel, Svenska Flottans Historia, Norrtälje 1903.

Where the Wasa capsized: between Beckholmen island and Tegelviken bay, May 1984.

The Wasa and
the King's Specifications

Anders Sandström

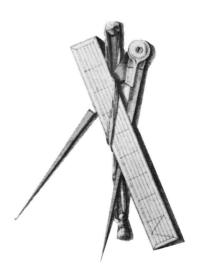

The Wasa and the Tre Kronor

One of the problems surrounding the *Wasa* concerns the reasons for her design and whether her measurement specifications were changed during her construction. Earlier students of this problem have presented the theory that the *Wasa* was enlarged on Royal orders when work on her construction had already started. This would have meant that the ship's draught became too shallow for the increased weight. On the basis of a comparison of the *Wasa's* size with that of the ship *Tre Kronor*, it has been concluded that the *Tre Kronor* was the first of the larger ships contracted by Henrik Hybertson in 1625 and that the *Wasa* was the second. The *Tre Kronor* and the *Wasa*, however, differ in size as well as in armament.[1] This comparison raises the question: "why was not the *Wasa* built according to the same specifications as the *Tre Kronor*, in accordance with the initial decision and contract?"

That the *Tre Kronor* and the *Wasa* were part of the same contract was first stated by Georg Hafström in an article in 1958[2]. The sources, upon which Hafström has based his conclusion, are the same that were later adopted by Björn Landström in his book *Vasan* (1980). One is the contract of January, 1625, which stipulates the delivery of a large ship in 1626, the second is the note in the shipyard records about the launching of the *Tre Kronor* in the autumn of 1625, and the final one is the actual delivery of the ship in 1626. This has led to the conclusion that the *Wasa* was to be of

Dividers, 17th century.

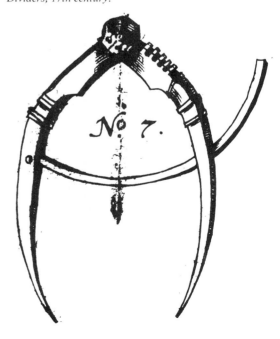

Dutch shipyard in the 17th century.

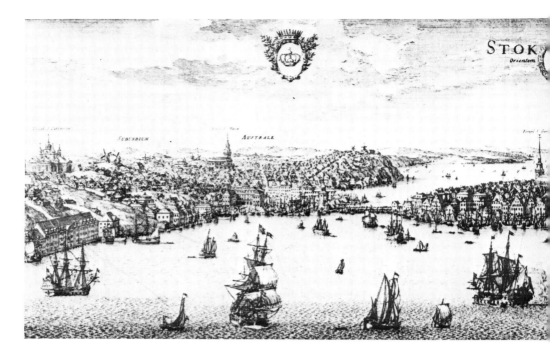

the same type as the *Tre Kronor*, but that she was later, on the orders of King Gustav Adolf, changed and enlarged.

The Wasa — Tre Kronor Connection

Is this reasoning correct? Is there any additional material that might throw light on the connection between the *Wasa* and the *Tre Kronor*? What did Henrik Hybertson's and Arendt de Groot's contract from 1625 actually contain?

Landström finds that the *Tre Kronor* was built "at record speed". This appraisal is based on the assumptions that Hybertson only after January started acquiring timber for the ship, launched it by the autumn and delivered it the following spring. If this is correct, the ship was certainly built in record time, as construction of a ship of this

size was normally two to three years. A more likely estimate, retroactive from the delivery time, is that the construction started 1624. At that time, the shipyard was leased by Antonius Monier, who employed Henrik Hybertson as Master Shipwright.

Monier's contract was signed during the autumn of 1620 and took effect from January, 1621. The contract period was five years, 1621—1625. During this period, Monier and Hybertson were to deliver three ships, "as large as the *Andromeda*". The first two ships were the *Maria* (1622) and the *Gustavus* (1624). Then in 1625, the ship *Mercurius* was delivered from the shipyard. Are these thus Monier's three ships? The next ship was the *Tre Kronor*, delivered in 1626. For all these ships, Hybertson was the Master Shipwright.

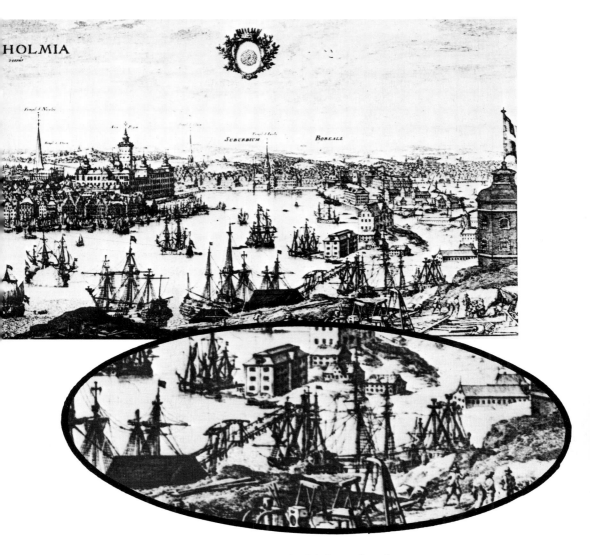

*Stockholm in the middle of the 17th century. To the right is an enlarged
detail of the Naval Yard. Drawing by Erik Dahlberg.*

The Naval Yard in the 1630's. Detail from a childhood portrait of Queen Kristina. The portrait is not signed, but was probably painted by J.H. Elbfas. To the left is the oldest Admiralty House, along the shore are the laid-up ships.

The Order Was Extended

There are, however, more factors to be considered. On February 25, 1622, another contract was signed with Monier and Hybertson, stipulating the construction of an additional ship. The contract said that the ship, which the contractors "now have under construction and according to the previous contract should have delivered to us" would be bought for cash by the Crown. Monier and Hybertson should, however, "nevertheless according to the previous contract produce as many ships and galleys and deliver them on time as they have promised".[3] Thus, altogether *four* ships were to be delivered during the contract period.

Hybertson's and de Groot's contract was signed in January, 1625, but did not become effective until January, 1626, when Monier's contract expired. The new contract included a clause that obliged Hybertson "to complete and fulfil according to the wording and content of the previous contract whatever is still missing upon the ships and vessels lying at the ship-yard".[4] From this point of view, it seems likely that, since the ship was not ready, Hybertson was ordered to complete it. The delay in fulfilling the contract is quite reasonable in view of the fact that one ship had been added.

The Length of the Contract Period

It thus seems to be the length of the contract periods which in earlier research created a misunderstanding about the *Tre Kronor — Wasa* connection. Hybertson's contract was written in January, 1625, but did not become effective until January, 1626.

Neither were the dimensions of the *Tre Kronor* known, except for one piece of information about her size (in lasts), requirement of canvas and the armament.[5] Her size is given as three hundred lasts and the number of guns as thirty, which indicates that she is a smaller ship than the *Wasa*, probably with only one gundeck. A close examination of the original material shows, however, that there is more information about the *Tre Kronor*, including the exact dimensions.

After the launching of the *Tre*

Launching in the Dutch manner. the Wasa was probably launched in this way. Dutch drawing from the 18th century.

Kronor in October of 1625, Master Henrik wanted instructions from the King as to whether he should start building one "large" ship or "2 such ships... as this is".[6] In a letter to the King in October, 1625, Klas Fleming states that the ship about to be launched (*Tre Kronor*) "has been built almost to the same pattern as the *Mercurius*, only that it will have a rounder bow".[7] The *Mercurius* was a ship of 230 lasts and with an armament of 32 guns.[8] These figures indicate a single-decker of considerably less dimensions than the *Wasa*.

Three Specifications

In the National Registry for the 30th of November, 1625, there is a specification for three ships. They have the following headings:

1. His Majesty's own specification for the ships that will be built
2. Master Henrik's specification for the ship which is now timbered in Stockholm
3. Paridon von Horn's specification for the ship which has been built in Västervik.

The specification is mentioned in *Svenska flottans historia* ("History of the Swedish Navy"), but without connection with any specific ship. It is possible to make any such connection? Fortunately, this can be done.

In a letter of October 3, 1625, Klas Fleming informs the King that "the new ship here at the yard has been completed so far that it can be launched within 3 weeks, and I enclose for Your Majesty a specification of how it has been built".[9] According to an entry in the shipyard archives, the *Tre Kronor* was launched in the end of October.[10] Thus, it is evident that Klas Fleming means the *Tre Kronor*. On the 4th of November, the King answers Klas Fleming. He acknowledges the receipt of "the specification by Master Henrik which you have sent us".[11] On November 30, the specification is entered in the National Registry as number 2. That this is really the case is confirmed by the continuation of the King's letter of November 4. He goes on to say that, having received Hybertson's specification, he has himself (the King) "carefully copied it and somewhat altered it ... desiring that you with Master Henrik agree that he construct the 2 smaller ships according to our enclosed specification and gives them a width in the bottom of the hold of 24 feet, about which nothing is mentioned in the specification sent here by you". In the specifications, entered in the National Registry on the 30th of November, 1625, the King's own specification has a bottom width of 24 feet, while there is no such measurement in Hybertson's specification. Thus, specification number 2 in the National Registry of the 30th of November, 1625, refers to the *Tre Kronor*. The size of the ship is best described by the keel length, which for the *Tre Kronor* is 108 feet and for the *Wasa* 135 feet.

It is not possible to use the same method in connecting specification number 3 to any particular ship. It might, however, be assumed that it is

The headings of the three specifications of November 30, 1625.

the *Svärdet*, built in Västervik in 1625 and taken over by the Crown in 1626. No other ship was completed in Västervik during this period.

Wasa — the First of Her Kind

Consequently, the *Wasa* was the first ship of its type. Some data from the archives are, however, difficult to interpret in this connection. In the autumn of 1624, the Admiralty was planning ship construction at the Naval Yard for the next few years. The following projects were planned:

Admiral Klas Fleming handled the contact between the King and the Master Shipwright Henrik Hybertson. Oil paiting by Lorentz Pasch the younger, Stockholm Municipal Court.

King Gustav II Adolf was personally engaged in the construction of the Wasa and drew up a specification of how the ship was to be built.

1626	one large ship, 136 feet long and 34 feet wide	1626	one large ship with a keel length of 64 "alns" and a width inside the planking of 17 "alns"
1627	one smaller ship		
1628	one large (equal with 1626) and	1628	one ship of equal size
1629	one smaller.	1629	two smaller ships (like the *Gustavus*).

On the 16th of January, 1625, the contract for the Yard was signed with Hybertson and Arendt de Groot. It specified the following deliveries:

The difference between this plan and the earlier one is that the smaller ship of 1627 has been moved forward to

1629. The measurements of the larger ships are approximately the same, notwithstanding the differing units of measure; one "aln" was equal to two feet, but the Amsterdam foot was somewhat shorter than the Swedish. Thus, 64 "alns" would be about 135 Amsterdam feet, while 17 "alns" would equal 34 Swedish feet. Also, the later list specifies the smaller ships — they are to be like the *Gustavus*. We may assume that this ship was of about the same size as the *Mercurius* and the *Tre Kronor*, measuring approx. 250 lasts, carrying 30 guns, having one gundeck and a keel length of about 108 feet.

If the *Tre Kronor* is not included in this plan, then the *Wasa* would be the first large ship of the two lists. How does this correspond with the actual delivery of the *Wasa* in 1628?

Completion of the Äpplet

The connection is more easily understood, if additional material is brought into the picture. On February 10, 1625, a new contract was signed with Master Henrik and Arendt de Groot. It concerned the completion of the ship *Äpplet*, built in the early 1620's. The construction of this ship had been started by Paridon von Horn and Christian Welshuisen in Västervik in 1618. When delivered in 1622, it was not fully completed. As it turned out, it was not sturdy enough to be used in naval service. According to the contract of February 1625, the keel, stem, stern and other essential parts would be strengthened. Also, the large stern cabins were to be built. Work was to start on April 1, 1625, and the ship was

to be delivered with the first ice-free water in the spring of 1626. The cost gives an idea of the scope of the project. It was estimated at 30.000 dalers[12], as compared to 40.000 dalers for each of the larger ships in the January contract.

The Naval Yard was thus faced with a considerably increased work load. Contracts had been signed for the delivery of almost two large ships within one year. We do not know the implications as far as the first contract is concerned; however, in a record from 1625/26, Master Henrik informs Klas Fleming that during 1625 he has ordered timber to be cut for one large ship and two smaller. This may lead to the conclusion that the work on the *Äpplet* forced one of the two larger ships to be cancelled or postponed.

Summary

On the basis of original material, available at the present time, we may conclude that the *Tre Kronor* was a smaller ship than the *Wasa*, Up till now, it has been assumed that the *Tre Kronor* was the first of the larger ships in the contract of 1625 and thus a sister ship of the *Wasa*. The question about the construction of the *Wasa* and the possible alterations, which may have been effected during the construction, must be viewed in this context. As an additional result of this study, we have been able to ascertain the dimensions of the *Tre Kronor*, hitherto unknown.

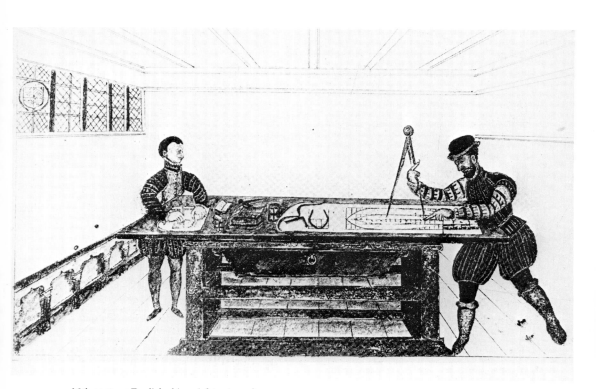

16th century English shipwrights at work.

"The King's Specification"

The contract for the *Wasa* was signed on January 16, 1625. One month later, the contract for the rebuilding of the *Äpplet* was signed. As a consequence of this, the first contract was probably changed from two large and two smaller ships into one large and two smaller ships. After the *Tre Kronor* had been launched in October, the keel for a new ship could be laid. According to the contract, this would be a large ship, with probable delivery in 1628. On September 20, however, the Navy lost ten ships in a storm off Domesnäs in Courland. This disaster was to influence the shipbuilding programme at the yard. On October 3, Klas Fleming reports that "the new ship" is ready to be launched within three weeks. Immediately after this, Master Henrik will lay the keel for a large ship or, if the King requests, he will "set up two such ships at the time, as this one is",[14]

On November 3, the King writes to the Council of State that the Council and the Nobility are to contribute money for the construction of two new ships, to be built by Master Henrik at the yard.[15] Next day, November 4, the King writes to Klas Fleming to inform him that he would rather see that Master Henrik "immediately sets up the two smaller

ships so that the number of ships will be filled sooner".[16] Now, the King is ready to revise the longterm planning and build the smaller ships first, as this would more quickly produce new ships in place of those lost. He wishes Fleming to enter into agreement "with Master Henrik to set up the two smaller ships according to our attached specification". He mentions the bottom width in his specification as 24 feet, which would indicate that the "attached specification" is the one entered into the National Registry for November 30. He also wishes Paridon von Horn to build three ships according to this specification. The length of the keel is to be 120 feet and the length of the sail beam 32 feet. This means that the size of the ship will be approximately between the *Tre Kronor* and the *Wasa*, i.e. between the sizes mentioned in the contract of January, 1625.

The Timber Not Suitable

As mentioned earlier, Henrik Hybertson had in 1625 ordered timber to be cut for one large and two smaller ships in accordance with the contract of January, 1625. He did not, however, consider that the new specification would match the cut timber. He could not build the 120 foot ship with the timber intended for the 136 foot ship "without detriment to himself".[17] On the other hand, neither could he build it with the timber intended for the smaller ships without problems. Apart from this, he declared himself willing to follow the King's specification as closely as possible. When Hybertson later made a closer survey of the cut timber, he found that it was sufficient for one large and one smaller ship.[18]

Master Henrik's objection in January that the timber did not match the King's specification annoyed the King. He ordered Fleming to make sure that ships were built according to the King's specification "or, if they are not willing or able to do so, that they set up that ship in the contract which is somewhat larger and have it completed at the soonest".[19] The King's letter resulted in Henrik Hybertson's being summoned to the Chancery on March 20. There, he was told to follow the King's order. He declared himself willing to do whatever he could, "in particular since Your

Stems, knees and other curved timbers were specially selected. Dimensions and angles were different for each ship.

Majesty has contracted with him earlier".[20] It was, however, possible that the ship "which is now under construction, will not be quite as large as Your Majesty's specification states".

How can we interpret this? To Landström, it confirms that the King required a ship, capable of carrying a sufficient number of 24 pounder guns.[21] Besides, he connects this with the *Wasa*; according to Landström, the specification pertains to the *Wasa*. Is this really so? Let us examine what information the original material can give us about the "King's specification" from October, 1625, to March, 1626.

Oct. 3   *1625.* Klas Fleming sends the King a specification for the ship which is to be launched within three weeks.

Nov. 4   *1625.* On the basis of a specification for the *Tre Kronor*, sent by Master Henrik, and Paridon von Horn's specification for a ship (the *Svärdet*?), the King has made a new specification, according to which he wishes the two smaller ships to be built.

Nov. 30   *1625.* The three specifications are entered into the National Registry. The King's new specification has a keel length of 120 feet.

Jan. 2   *1626.* Master Henrik declares that the timber he has cut does not match the King's specification. This applies to the timber intended for the contracted smaller as well as for the contracted larger ship. Thus, the ship envisaged by the specification has a length of somewhere between 108 and 135 feet. It ought to be the 120 foot specification from November 30.

Feb. 22   *1626.* The King replies to the letter of January 2, and orders Master Henrik to build the ship according to the specification. He adds that, if he is not willing to build according to the specification, he may build the contracted larger ship (i.e. 135 feet). It seems that the specification in question is still the one for a 120 foot ship.

March 21 1626. As a result of this letter, Master Henrik is summoned to the Chancery and advised of the King's wishes. He declares himself willing to do whatever he can to fulfill what has earlier been contracted, but the ship now under construction will not be as large as the specification.

The specification discussed on March 21 still appears to be the one for a 120 foot ship — it is the King's views from February 22 which are conveyed to Master Henrik when the letter has reached Stockholm. No new specification can be involved. The reason why the ship will not be quite as large as the specification states is possibly the one given by Master Henrik already on January 2; the timber was intended for a somewhat smaller ship, probably with a keel length of about 108 feet, as the *Tre Kronor*. It is perfectly reasonable for him not to use the timber intended for the 135 foot ship, as this was to be built eventually, even if the sequence was reversed.

The Domesnäs disaster thus caused a temporary revision of the long-term shipbuilding programme. In order to get new ships as quickly as possible, the King decided to postpone the larger ships, and instead build the smaller first. However, he wanted to draw up the specification for the new ships personally. This he did by requesting information concerning the two ships then ready in Stockholm and Västervik. On this information he based the specification for the 120 foot ships, which he wanted built in Stockholm and Västervik. The procedure gives an interesting insight into the King's personal interest in strengthening the Navy.

The King's Requirements

What does this mean for the planning and construction of the *Wasa*? The ship that the King wanted to be built was an enlarged version of the *Tre Kronor*. An interesting figure in the specification gives the height between the "orlops" (Swedish: "överlopp") as 6 1/2 feet. This measure is missing, both in the specification from Stockholm and the one from Västervik. "Överlopp" in the language of the day meant gundeck, which might indicate that the enlarged "smaller" ships were intended to have two gundecks. This, however, is subject to some doubt;

all three specifications give the number of gunports as 24. A ship with two gundecks would of course have a larger number of gunports.

On March 20, Hybertson reports that the ship now under construction will not be as big as the specification said, that is a keel length of 120 feet. This might mean that he has already started to build the small ship by this time. A possible further development of the project could be that he then lengthened the keel to 135 feet and continued by building the larger ship.

Three Scarf Joints

Landström finds it peculiar that the keel of the *Wasa* has three scarf joints. If the length of the *Wasa's* keel is measured from the stern end up to and including the third keel timber, it will be 111 feet. The fourth keel timber gives a total length of 135 feet. A possible hypothesis would then be that Hybertson on March 20, 1626, laid the keel for the 120 foot ship. As the timber was not meant for such a large ship, he could not assemble a longer keel than about 111 feet, which explains his comment that the ship will not be quite as big as the specification. When the King then permits him to build the larger ship instead, he lengthens the keel with one more timber. The result is a keel of four scarfed timbers. This explanation is also supported by the fact that the keel of the *Wasa* is fairly thin in relation to its length.

No Wasa Specification

The specification for the *Wasa* has

never been found. The circumstances around the construction of the *Wasa*, related above, lead to the question whether there ever existed any specification for the *Wasa*, approved by the King. During the six months prior to the construction of the *Wasa*, the 120 foot specification, put forward by the King, has been in force. In his letter of February 22, the King allows Hybertson to disregard the "specification" and instead build a larger ship "according to the contract". The contract only specifies length and width.

The Inquiry

At the inquiry after the disaster, when Hybertson has already died, his successor Hein Jacobsen answers that he built it according to the "instruction, which had been given to him by Master Henrik and on His Majesty's orders". Then Hybertson's brother and partner Arendt de Groot mentions that the ship was built in accordance with a Dutch prototype, approved by the King. Hafström has strongly questioned whether this statement is reasonable; in all likelihood de Groot was in Holland and saw the ship only after the construction of the *Wasa* had started.[22]

The above can be summarized as follows: when Hybertson gets permission from the King to build the contracted larger ship, he himself draws up a specification, based on his experience as a shipbuilder. This becomes the "instruction" which Hein Jacobsen is to follow. Later in the same interrogation, Arendt de Groot mentions that the King had

known and approved the length and width of the ship. This agrees with the hypothesis that the ship was built on the basis of the dimensions, laid down in the contract of January, 1625, with the exception that Jacobsen on his own initiative widened the ship by five inches. The original material never mentions any "specification" in connection with the *Wasa*. Thus, it is reasonable to assume that no specification was ever made; the *Wasa* was built according to a work description drawn up by Henrik Hybertson.

Björn Landström "on strong circumstantial evidence" finds King Gustav Adolf quilty of causing the *Wasa* to be built too large. He guesses that the King, having learnt that a ship with two gundecks was being built in Denmark, ordered the *Wasa* to be enlarged. As is shown above, this is not correct. From the autumn of 1625 to the spring of 1626, the King was interested in the rapid construction of smaller ships. The reason why this preference did not materialize is rather, with a more likely interpretation of the original material, that during 1625, Henrik Hybertson had collected timber for the ships envisaged in the contract of January, 1625. This timber was less suitable for the smaller ships of the King's specification.

The Sister Ship of the Wasa

Finally, another comment: earlier studies have assumed that the *Tre Kronor* was a sister ship of the *Wasa*. We have seen that this was not the case. However, the contract of 1625 speaks of two large ships. Were two ships built, and which one was in that case the real sister ship of the *Wasa*? What has been said above leads us to conclude that this ship ought to have been built after the *Wasa*. Nothing is said at the inquiry after the *Wasa* disaster which suggests any comparison with any ship built earlier according to the same contract as the *Wasa*. But during the inquiry, a comment is made, which is interesting in this respect. In the discussion about the construction of the *Wasa*, Söfring Hansson, her Captain, says: "I fear that the same thing will happen to the ship which Hein Jacobsen is now building, as it is being built in the same way". Thus, the sister ship of the *Wasa* was under construction at the yard, when the *Wasa* capsized. One hypothesis is that this was the *Nyckeln*, completed at the Naval Yard in 1630. And what happened to the sister ship of the *Wasa*? The *Nyckeln* served in the Navy for many years: she was more fortunate than the *Wasa*.

NOTES

1. *Sveriges sjökrig 1611—1632 ("Naval Wars of Sweden 1611—1632")* p.34.
2. Hafström, Georg. Örlogsskeppet Wasas undergång 1628 ("The Wreck of the Warship Wasa, 1628") *Tidskrift i Sjöväsendet* 1958, p.741.
3. *Contract- och arrendebok för år 1622 (Contract and Lease Book for the Year 1622")* Naval Yard Records, Kammararkivet.
4. *Contract- och arrendebok för år 1625 ("Contract and Lease Book for the Year 1625")* Naval Yard Records, Kammararkivet.
5. *Sveriges sjökrig 1611—1632*, p. 251. *Sjöhistorisk årsbok ("Yearbook of Maritime History")* 1963—64, pp. 39 ff.
6. Klas Fleming to Gustav Adolf October 3, 1625. National Archives.
7. Ibid.
8. *Sveriges sjökrig*, p. 244.
9. Same as note 6.
10. Räkenskapsbok (Account Book) for 1625. Naval Yard Records, Kammararkivet.
11. Riksregistraturet (National Registry), November 4, 1625.
12. Same as note 4.
13. *Svenska flottans historia ("History of the Swedish Navy")*, 1:2, p. 236.
14. *Sveriges sjökrig*, p. 23, note.
15. *Sveriges sjökrig*, p. 34.
16. Same as note 11.
17. Klas Fleming to Gustav Adolf, January 2, 1626. National Archives.
18. Klas Fleming to Gustav Adolf, February, 1626. National Archives.
19. Gustav Adolf to Axel Oxenstierna, February 22, 1626, *Axel Oxenstiernas brev ("Letters of Axel Oxenstierna")*, 2:1, pp. 303 f.
20. Kammarens registratur (Chancery Registry), March 21, 1626.
21. Landström, Björn, *Vasan*, 1980, p. 48.
22. Hafström, Georg, *Utblickar kring tillkomsten av skeppet Wasa, ("Aspects on the Origins of the Ship Wasa")*, 1968, p. 84.

WASA STUDIES

1. Barkman, Lars, *Konserveringen av Wasa*, 1962 (For English translation, see Study no. 5).
2. Lundström, Per, *Utgrävningen av Wasa* (*"The Excavation of the Wasa"*), 1962.
3. Hafström, Georg, *Några problem kring regalskeppet Wasa* (*"Some Problems about the Warship Wasa"*), 1963.
4. Howander, B, Åkerblad, H, *Wasavarvet i Stockholm* (*"The Wasa Museum in Stockholm"*), 1963.
5. Barkman, Lars, *The Preservation of the Wasa*, 1965.
6. Barkman, Lars, *On Resurrecting a Wreck*, 1967.
7. Barkman, Lars, *Repliker av reliker* (*"Replicas of Relics"*), 1969.
8. Bengtsson, Sven, *The Sails of the Wasa*, 1975.
9. Hamilton, E, and Sandström, A, *Sjöstrid på Wasas tid* (*"Naval Fighting at the Time of the Wasa"*), 1982.
10. Kaijser, I, Nathorst-Böös, E, and Persson, I-L, *Ur sjömannens kista och tunna* (*"From the Sailor's Chest and Barrel"*), 1982.
11. Skenbäck, Urban, *Sjöfolk och knektar på Wasa* (*"Sailors and Soldiers on the Wasa"*), 1981.